Published by Adam X. Hearn
Copyright © Adam X. Hearn

Artwork and design
by Gabriel Rosado

2008

www.thebookofpeaceandlove.com

AUTHORS PLEDGE

I pledge to give 50% of the profits of this book to organisations that help to promote peace and love worldwide. For more details or to nominate an organisation for consideration please visit the website: **www.thebookofpeaceandlove.com**

WHAT IS THIS BOOK FOR?

The idea behind this book is that in order for there to be peace and love in the world we have to ask for peace and love, and to do this we need to be able to communicate with the whole of humanity. When writing this book I discovered the power of asking for peace and love as I asked literally hundreds of people around the world to teach me how to say and how to write Peace and Love in their languages. It is truly transformational and an exercise that I would recommend to everyone. Try it, next time you hear someone speaking in a language you don't understand, and see how they react. For some, peace and love are a serious matter, and answers are given with great solemnity. For the majority, teaching these words to another is a small step towards **sharing our deeper humanity,** and those moments in time they share with you will be accompanied by smiles, joy, perhaps laughter at unbelievable mispronunciation!

This is truly Word Magic, it is a way of building bridges between people on a deep subconscious level, of crossing divides that are as illusory as we wish them to be.

This book encompasses only a small fraction of the nearly 7000 languages spoken on our planet. If you flick through and don't find your language then please see this as a great opportunity. I would ask you to write in and share your language with us, and if you can, try to share it with as many other people on the planet as possible.

The languages that have been included are there simply because I have managed to come in contact with them on my travels, and for no political or ideological purpose. They are not in any particular order nor are they associated with any particular place as **language trascends borders.**

NOTE: The words and pronunciations herein are only some of the many alternative ways of saying peace and love in different languages. Some cultures use alternatives frequently, and we welcome any feedback about alternatives. We apologise in advance for any mistakes.

With gratitude to the literally hundreds of wonderful people around the world who have helped me to nourish a small seed into a beautiful tree of Peace and Love, this book is for you all.

Dedicated in memory of my younger brother, Orlando Konrad Hearn who taught me so much about Peace and Love.

SPANISH

Paz y Amor

(Paath eee Amor)

FRENCH

Paix et Amour

(Pay et Amah)

PORTUGUESE

Paz y Amor

(pass eee amoh)

GERMAN

Frieden und Liebe

(Free-den und Lee-ber)

ITALIAN

Pace e Amore

(Pa-chey ee amo-rey)

POLISH

pokój i miłość

(pok-ooee ee mee-washed-ch)

GREEK

Eiphnh qe Agapi

ειρήνη και αγαπώ

(iti-rini kay agap-ee)

LITHUANIAN

Ramybė Meile

(ramee beh my-ee-lee)

ROMANIAN

Pace şi Dragoste

(patchey dzi dragostay)

SLOVENIAN

Pokoj ter Ljubezen

(pokoy ter lyubeshen)

CZECH

Mír a Láska

(Meer alas carr)

SERBIAN

Mir pa Ljubav
(Mir pah luyoobov)

SLOVAK

Mier a Láska

(Mierr alas carr)

DUTCH

Vrede en Liefde

(frede en leef day)

ALBANIAN

Paqe e Dashuri

(packeh ey dashuri)

LATVIAN

Miers un Mīlulis

(miers oon miloolish)

HUNGARIAN
(MAGYARÚL)

Béke és Szerelem

(baykay is sherelem)

CROATIAN

Mir i Hatar

(mir ee hatar)

NORWEGIAN/DANISH

Fred og Elske
(Fred og elsker)

SWEDISH

Fred och Älska

(Fred och elska)

ALBANIAN

Paqe e Dua
(pack-ay ay dua)

FINNISH

Rauhaa ja Rakkautta
(Ra-woo har ear rack out aah)

ESTONIAN

Rahu ja Armastust

(rahoo ear armah stust)

MACEDONIAN

Mir I Ljubov

(Meer ee ljoobov)

GAELIC

Suíocháin agus Grá

she-hjorn ogus graw
(to rhyme with draw)

ICELANDIC

Friður og ást

(Free-ur og est)

UKRAINIAN

мир и Любов

(mee-rr lee-oobov)

TURKISH

BARIŞ ve SEVGİ

(BAR-eeesh vey SEV-Ghee)

RUSSIAN

мир и любовь

mir l ljubov

(me-er eee lyoo-bov)

NORTHERN SAMI

Ráfi ja Ráhkesvuohta

(Raff-ee yah ra-kesvuota)

ARABIC

(hab na salaaam)

UYGHUR

Tinchliq Küyünüx
(Tink-lick kayay-nicks)

TURKMEN

Parahatçylyk Soygi

(Parahat-cheeleek Soy-ghee)

PERSIAN/FARSI

عشق و صلح

(Eshgh va Solh)

HEBREW

אהבה (ע"ש)
(shalom v'ahar-war)

ARMENIAN

Խաղաղություն
և
սեր

(jh-a-gh-a gh-u tsioon yev s e r)

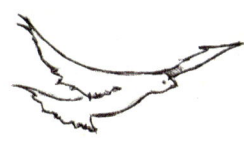

CEBUANO

Kalinaw Matahum

(kali-now matahumm)

YIDDISH

Friden in libshaft

(Frid-den in lib-shaft)

BENGALI

শান্তি এবং ভালবাসা

Shanti ebong Bhalobasha

(shanti ebong balobasher)

HINDI

अमन चाह

(shanti or pyar)

OR

अमन और प्रेम

(Aman or Prem)

MARATHI

शांती आणि प्रेम
Shaa-nti aani prem

(shan-tea aani prem)

NEPALI

शान्ति र माया

shanti ra maya

(shantee rah mayar)

JAPANESE

平和
と
愛

(Heiwa doh eye)

MANDARIN

和平與愛

he-ping yu ai

(hey-ping yu ai)

KOREAN

안녕 와사랑

Sarang Pthyongh'wa

(sarang feeyongwar)

JAVANESE

Perdamaian dan Mencintai

(Perdama-yan dan mencint-ay)

VIETNAMESE

Hòa Bình và Tình Yêu

(Ho-ah bin var tin you)

THAI

สันติภาพ และ ความรัก

Santiphap le kwamra

(Santee-fap le kwamrah)

LAO

San-ti-phab lai Khouam-hak

(santeefap lay-ee koo-oo am- hak)

MALAY

Keamanan Cinta

(kia-manan sintar)

TAGALOG

Kapayapaan at Pagmamahal

(kapayapaan at pag-mamahal)

MAORI

Nohopuku Mä Aroha

(nohopuku ma arohar)

KHMER

សន្តិភាព ស្រលាញ់

Son ti pheap Sror lagn

(Son-tea feep sroar lann)

AZERBAIJIAN AZERI

sakitlik isæ istæmæk

(sakitlik is-ay eestay-make)

SINHALESE

Samaya saha Adaraya

(saa ma ya sa ha aa da ra ya)

TLINGIT

Yux' See H'un
Yux See Hun

(yajjjj si jjjan)

PUNJABI

ਅਮਨ ਤੇ ਪਯ

Amn pyar

(Am Pee-Yar)

URDU

امن و امان

Aman o Aaman

(a-man or aah-man)

TAMIL

Amaithi Virumpukirén

(am I tea, virumpuk-iren)

TIBETAN

ཞི་བདེ་དགའ་པོ་

Zhibde Dga'po

(shib-day degap-ooh)

BAHASA INDONESIA

Damai Kasih

(Damai kasih)

QUETCHUA

Sumac Kuyay

(Soomac Koo-ya-ee)

INUKTITUT (INUIT)

ᓴᐃᒪᓂᖅ ᓇᒡᓕᒍᓱᖕᓂᕐᓗ

Saimaniq Nagligusungnirlu

(Sa-ee-manic Nag-lee goo sung nir-loo)

HOPI

Sipala Naugula

(Sipalah now-goolah)

CHEYENNE

nanomonestôtse naa méhót

(Nanomone stutse na me-hott)

CHEROKEE

ᏅᏩᏙᎯᏯᏛ ᎬᎨᏳᎢ

nv-wa-do-hi-ya-dv gv-ge-yu-i

(nuh wah doe he yaw
duh guh gay you ee)

HAWAIAN

Aloha eia Malu

(Alohar eia maloo)

RAPA NUI

Kiba-kiba Hanga
(Keeba-keeba hanger)

LUO

Kwe gi Hera
(Kway ghee herah)

KIKUYU

Hayu na Gikeno

(Hayoo na gikeno)

CHICHEWA, CHEWA, CHINYANJA

Mutendere na cikondi

(moo-tenderay na seekondee)

NUER

Mäl kän nog
(Mell kennog)

FANTE

Asomdwee no odo

(Asomdwh'eh na od'oh)

KAMBA

Muuwo na Wendo

(moo-woh na wendoh)

MAASAI

Enyora ta-lowe Osotwa

(enyorah ta-lowey osotwar)

AKWA IBOM, IBIBIO, EFIK, OGOJA

Emem ye Ima

(Emem yey imar)

EDO

Ofome I Homoegbe
(Ofom-ay ee homoeggbay)

HAUSA

Salamu Lumaana Kaunaa

(salamoo lumahnah ka-oonah)

YORUBA

Ifé ati Alafia

(ee-fay atee alafia)

IBO/IGBO

Udo na Ihunanya

(udo nah ihoonanyah)

IGEDE

Okfungi bala Ohaha
(Okfungee balah ohaha)

IDOMA

Ebó Ihotu

(Ebb-oh! Ee hotoo)

SOMALI

Nabad iyo Jeclaansho

(nabad ee-yo jay-clanshow)

MALAGASY

Fitiavana amana Fandriampahalemana

(fitiavana amana fandriampa-halemanah)

SHONA

Rugare na Rudo

(roogareh nah roodo)

ZULU

ukuthula no thando

(Ukutoola no t-hando)

SESOTHO

Lerato le Hothula

(Lerato ley hooee-toolah)

SETSWANA

Kagiso le Lorato

(kagiso lay loratoh)

LUGANDA

Mirembo No Kwagala

(mirembo no kwagalah)

ATESO

Ajokus na akwap Kebe Amina

(Ajokus na ak-wap kaybay aminar)

RUNYORO-RUTORO

Obusinge Ne Engonzi
(obusingah neh engo-see)

RUNYANKORE-RUKIGA

Obusingye Na Rukundo

(Obusingay nah rukundo)

SWAHILI

Amani na Upendo

(ama-nee nah oo-pendo)

LUGBARA

Asi Anzu Lepa
(Ass-ee an-zoo leper)

AMHARIC

ፍቅር ና ሰላም

Fiki ena Selam

(Feekee enah se-lam)

KINYARWANDA

Amahoro na Ndakunda

(Amahorow nah enda-kunda)

XHOSA

Utando no Kuthula

(Ootando no Kootoolah)

WOLOF

Mbugeel Jaama
(Mbug-eel jaamah)

LUSOGA

Miraala Ne Kugonza

(Miraalah ney kugonza)

ICIBEMBA

Icibote ne Citemwiko

(Itchi botey neh see-temwikoh)

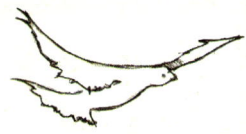

LINGALA

Kimia na Bolingo

(Kimiar nah bolingo)

ESPERANTO

Paco kaj Ami

(Paco kay amee)

The following pages are blank for you to add in peace and love in any other languages you come across. There are nearly 7000 languages spoken today, so you may need some more space.

If you would like to have a language included in the forthcoming Big Book of Peace and Love, then please write in with details.

www.thebookofpeaceandlove.com